CU00971232

Man-trailing

Man-trailing

How to train your bloodhound

Christiane Liebeck

Copyright © 2008 by Cadmos Verlag GmbH, Brunsbek
Design: Ravenstein + Partner, Verden
Typesetting: Nadine Hoenow
Photos: Lehari, Mozarski, Freier
Print: agensketterl Druckerei, Mauerbach

All rights reserved.

Copying or storing in electronic or any other form is not
permitted without the written agreement of the publisher.

Published in Austria

ISBN 978-3-86127-929-7

Table of contents

Preface 8
    Acknowledgements 9

Introduction 1 1
    What is man-trailing?..12
        The difference between tracking and man-trailing..12
    For whom is man-trailing interesting? 14
        Professional man-trailers..15
    Which dog is best suited?..17

Basic knowledge 19
    The dog's world of perception 19
    Anatomy and function of the dog's nose..21
    What is smell?...23
        Skin scales 25
        The diffusion of the individual smell 26
        Interference by environmental factors..27
        Development and diffusion of the trail..28

Training preparations 30
    The equipment required 30
        The dog's harness 30
        The trailing lead 31
        Indications 31
        Plastic bags for scent articles 32
        Water bottle for the dog...32
        Jackpot for the dog 33
        Safety equipment for handler and dog 33
        Other useful items 33
    Scent articles 34
        Correct handling of the scent article 36

Table of contents

The trail-layer and his job 37
     Indications 37
     Helpers and companions 38
Training documentation 39
Handling of the lead 41
The pre-scent 43
The start 44
     The starting command 45
     Command language 47
Reward after work 49
Identification 50
Training on an indicated trail 51
Team training on a non-indicated trail 54
Basic trail 55

Training programme 58
Training structure basics 58
Absolute beginners 59
Beginners 66
Advanced learners 67
Summary 69

What does the dog tell us on a trail? 70
Body language and body expressions 70
Negative indication on the trail 72

Table of contents

Circling at the beginning of the trail 73
Circling on the trail 73
The zigzag assessment 74
Wavy lines 74
The head-turn 76
Tail carriage 78
Working old and fresh trails 78

How to continue 80
Recovering a trail 80
Recovery of a trail 82
Scent pool 82
Implementation in an emergency 84
Crossing and splitting 86
Backtrack 88
Line-up 89
Negative indication at the beginning and the end of a trail............................90
Contamination 91

The essentials in brief 93

Bibliography 96

Preface

Nose work with dogs is becoming increasingly popular. Anyone who plays nose games with his dog will know that the dog achieves amazing results with his sense of smell. Nose games offer a practical challenge that is great fun for both people and dogs.

Drug dogs, bomb detection dogs, tracking dogs and square-search dogs – to name just a few – are known for police work, as well as search-and-rescue work. Man-trailing as a search method, in contrast, has been rarely written about.

Those interested in man-trailing have so far had to rely on tediously finding individual articles from different resources. In some books the subject is mentioned, but no detailed and complete handbook has been available until now.

With this book I give you the chance to immerse yourself in a world that we can't perceive with our eyes – as the dog smells what we can't see.

"Man-trailing" means that the dog is searching for the individual smell of a person.

In the United States and in some European countries, this form of search work is already practised by the police and aid organizations and it's through this that the bloodhound is mainly known. You may remember film scenes where bloodhounds were used to search for missing persons and to pursue criminals. In Germany, dogs are also trained for this kind of search work for the police and for aid organizations.

Anyone who would like to keep their dog fit and healthy and offer him practical and challenging work can use nose work at home too.

Some dogs are unchallenged during their daily walks – the physical exercise isn't enough for them – and the dog needs mental stimulation in order to fall into his basket tired and happy after work. With nose work the dog has a problem to solve that makes a routine walk much more varied – and not just for the dog.

As soon as you and your dog have an understanding of man-trailing you will be surprised at what he can achieve. Working with you he will become a high achiever, as any kind of nose work is perfectly suited for occupying and working a dog.

This book is intended to be a handbook that provides basic instruction in man-trailing and gives an understanding of the fascinating work of the dog. It will not turn every dog into a search-and-rescue dog automatically – the objective is the occupation of the dog and above all the enjoyment of the owner with his dog.

I hope you enjoy reading the book and above all wish you happy trailing!

Acknowledgements

At this point I would first like to thank my husband Oliver, who has always supported and encouraged me in writing this book up to the point of its completion. I would like to thank my friend Dr Maren Neumann-Aukthun, who has lent me an ear, and not just in the area of veterinary matters. Many thanks also go to my friend Annette Freier, who has had considerable experience with her two dogs and has shared it with me.

Other people as well as dogs have also contributed to the development of this book. In seminars and training sessions I gained considerable experience. Special thanks go to

The two scenthounds, Tos and Cana, are always keen and persistent at their work. (Photo: Lehari)

Robin and Kevin Kocher from the United States, who "polished" the book. Their encouragement and support helped with its development. Their accumulated experiences and the right to use their papers have allowed me to present the subject of man-trailing.

Last but not least I thank my two scenthounds, Tos and Cana, who bring joy and persistence to their work with me.

Introduction

A puzzle is fragmented into many individual pieces. By putting those individual pieces together correctly you get the whole picture that might, for example, show a living being or a landscape. If one piece is missing, the picture is incomplete. Man-trailing as an "overall picture" also consists of many pieces that only add to a successful man-trailing team as a whole.

Every chapter of this book can therefore be labelled as piece of the puzzle – which means every single element. It's very important to understand every element in order to be able to put it into practice in training. Training must be suited to the stage of development and the needs of the dog. Gaps in training and problems caused by unrealistic demands can only be poorly "patched" during the later process. Consequently this will often cause problems when working the trail.

The word "man-trailing" doesn't appear in the dictionary. It's simply a technical expression to describe the dog's job: following a human trail. In this book the expressions "man-trailing" and "trailing" are used synonymously. People doing this job with their dog are called "man-trailers".

Training starts with the basics, and only with a thoroughly designed training plan will the team be successful. In addition, the handler needs the right instinct, as he is working with a living being. Always remember that a successful man-trailing team can only exist on a soundly built basis.

What is man-trailing?

In seminars, continuing education or simply when talking to different dog owners, I keep realizing that there is no notional differentiation of the term "man-trailing". Man-trailing is often mentioned in the same breath as tracking. In the beginning this led to notional confusion for me. So as not to confuse you with this I would like to highlight the difference between these search methods. This is particularly important for the man-trailing training, as the two methods differ significantly.

The difference between tracking and man-trailing

When tracking, the dog follows the scent particles of disturbed earth. Those particles originate in the crushed vegetation and disturbed earth that a foot, for example, leaves when walking. It makes no difference to the dog whether the disturbed earth was caused by human footprints or with mechanical devices such as a car tyre, for instance. The dog has learned to follow the scent of disturbed earth. The tracking course should be followed with the head held low and the nose should always be close to the track on the ground.

Man-trailing is the pursuit of the individual scent trail that every person leaves behind, just like a fingerprint. With the aid of an article that is thoroughly contaminated with the missing person's scent, the man-trailing dog is able to filter out the right trail from all the scents of different people and the surrounding environment.

The dog works in wooded and open areas as well as on asphalt in the middle of a city – anywhere that the environment is mixed with the individual scent. The individual scent gives the dog the information it needs to follow the trail.

What scent is and how scent and trail act are explained precisely in the section "What is smell?".

Tracking is the pursuit of the combined scent of crushed vegetation and organisms in the ground. Man-trailing is the pursuit of the individual scent of a sought-after person.

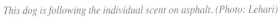

This dog is following the individual scent on asphalt. (Photo: Lehari)

During training it's always beneficial if a good man-trailer can share his experiences. (Photo: Lehari)

For whom is man-trailing interesting?

Originally dogs were used as helpers for humans. They were supposed to go "to work" with the people, whether this was hunting or herding sheep.

Nowadays for many people they are partners and family dogs nobody wants to be without.

It's beneficial to the well-being of any dog to find an appropriate form of activity for him. Nose work, therefore, is very popular. The dog's nose is its most highly developed sense. Every dog searches with its nose or follows different tracks with it. Hunting dogs can easily follow a deer track, and a male is able to trace a female in heat over many kilometres.

The drive to follow things is diverted to the human trail in training a man-trailing dog. It's not about motivating him to go hunting, but letting him follow a trail laid by us. The dog's hunting instinct is satisfied by an alternative activity.

Man-trailing is an enjoyable activity that works the dog not just physically but also, more importantly, mentally. When practised as a leisure activity, it provides recreation and the fun of the handler and the dog working as a team. Also, you will be astonished to see what tasks your dog can perform. The shared enjoyment and activity makes some dogs easier to handle and an otherwise ordinary walk turns into an adventure for both handler and dog.

Any dog can learn the basics of man-trailing irrespective of age. Your dog will thank you for giving him a job to do.

And who knows, if you are dedicated enough, your team may achieve the ultimate outcome and turn "pro".

Professional man-trailers

Instruction for professional purposes includes very time-consuming and intensive training. In an emergency, the goal is to save a human life or to pursue a criminal, after all. Man-trailing can also be useful in an investigation. Whether a man-trailing team is successful depends on many factors. Handler and dog have to be physically fit and healthy, as they have to walk not only through the city for kilometres but also cross-country through fields and woods.

The dog handler should have a good knowledge of cynology and be able to understand and interpret his dog's individual behaviour and his body language properly. These skills

Even a puppy can be encouraged at an early age and will be well prepared for professional man-trailing later on. (Photo: Lehari)

are essential, as a man-trailing team can only survive in practice through correct interpretation and application.

Knowing what scent is, how it is affected by environmental influences and how it acts are also basic requirements. The handling and use of technical equipment such as a compass and walkie-talkie are part of the basic training, as is the reading and practical use of maps and plans.

Don't rest on your laurels. Training must be continued throughout the dog's man-trailing career and will keep presenting new challenges.

For the police, man-trailing is inevitably an important way of searching for criminals. There are many different operational areas where a man-trailer can give support and useful advice in solving crimes.

In the United States, man-trailing dogs are already used by the police quite often. (Photo: Mozarski)

Example of a professional man-trailer
A shop in a city shopping centre was robbed at night. As he was leaving the shop the robber lost his cap. There were no witnesses and no signs of the robber's whereabouts. A man-trailer was put onto the robber's lost cap onsite. The trained man-trailing dog was able to filter out the individual smell of the robber from all the existing smells and to pick up and follow the trail.

For professional work the training of a puppy as a man-trailing dog has its advantages. The puppy's predispositions can be encouraged and directed early on. For a solid basic education three or four training days a week are necessary. Training sessions must take place at different times of the day.

Only through these learning experiences and growing maturity can a good man-trailing team develop. And I'm not just talking about the dog. The person at the other end of the lead is just as important as his trail partner.

Whenever an abandoned or stolen car is found that could have been used by a criminal, it's possible to let the man-trailer pick up the smell from the car seat. In this case the car seat is the scent article and the dog can therefore filter out the starting point of the runaway and follow it.

When the starting point of a sought-after person is known, the man-trailer can be put onto it to identify his direction. In the city the mantrailer can follow the person's track. A man-trailing team working for an aid organization's canine unit is a great help and support in quickly finding missing people. Then there is the field of application of search-and-rescue organizations, which are called to rescue operations to search for the missing.

From my own experience and talking to other skilled trainers I can say that the road to becoming an operational man-trailing team can be quite a rocky one. Real-life operations are individual and invariably throw up new, unexpected situations for which you are untrained. In this event a strongly bonded man-trailing team is necessary in order to be able to do sound professional work.

It's advisable to train the dog in the field of man-trailing only, as this is the only way to develop his expertise in this area.

Which dog is best suited?

Man-trailing is mainly known through bloodhounds, which achieve remarkable performances. Dog owners who handle a bloodhound in man-trailing swear by this breed. They possess excellent skills and the best olfactory performance for the field of man-trailing.

Nowadays, however, many other breeds are trained in man-trailing and also achieve brilliant results, although certain breeds fulfil the olfactory performance qualification better than others. Here genetics, intelligence and training play an important role.

Hunting dogs certainly are among those breeds with the best qualities for man-trailing work. Any dog that likes to use his nose in everyday life is especially well suited and will be easy to interest in man-trailing. But it is only through regular and consistent training that the functionality of the memory and the nose's ability to discriminate are improved.

The bloodhound is said to possess the best olfactory performance of all dogs and is therefore often used in man-trailing. (Photo: Mozarski)

Other breeds will also have their advantages and disadvantages for this kind of work. The important thing is that you as the dog handler consider the individual pros and cons to find the right dog for yourself. At this point I would like to say that there is no such thing as the perfect man-trailing dog. Every dog has its strengths and weaknesses. It's important to recognize these and use them properly when searching. There are dogs that show impressive performances in the city; others trail confidently in open areas.

This bloodhound is hard at work on the trail. (Photo: Mozarski)

Basic knowledge

The dog's world of perception

My dogs have settled in the garden with out-stretched legs. They are warming themselves in the sunshine with their eyes half-closed. Apparently out of nowhere, one of the dogs jumps up, its nose held up in the air with the nostrils mov-ing constantly. What's going on now? I can't see or hear anything. But there must be something in the air.

Dogs live in a different sensory world and have the ability to perceive their environment intense-ly and orientate themselves using their extraor-dinary sense of smell. For them, smells have a much higher and different significance than for

Smells that the dog can perceive and differentiate simultaneously. (Photo: Mozarski)

● *Car emissions* ● *Children's food*
● *Child* ● *Two children*
○ *Butcher's shop*

we humans. They use their sense of smell for information gathering, for sexual instinct and for orientation. Smells arouse different instincts in dogs.

When the dog smells something there is usually an automatic strong emotional response. "Fragrance" means something quite different for humans and dogs. A dog won't experience the sense of well-being that we feel when smelling a pleasant perfume.

The dog's sense of smell never seems to be overloaded and he never seems to be bored during walks as long as he can rummage. Even if the evening walk is always on the same route he seems to explore it over and over again.

In the world of smells the dog far outperforms us. Humans can only imagine the gigantic and manifold world of smells he is living in.

In humans the eye is the principal sensory organ. It picks up pictures and passes them across to the optic nerve. Through different colours in all kinds of nuances that we perceive we can evaluate what we see and where we are. Something similar happens with the dog's sense of smell. As principal sensory organ it picks up smells and subdivides them into a large number of individual perceptions. Humans are not able to do this. The dog "smells in pictures", which the olfactory nerve subdivides in the brain in the way that the human eyes process the visual information.

Smells can be perceived over kilometres, where the human vision isn't good enough. In darkness a dog can easily orientate itself with its nose. From its point of view the dog is able to 'see' through forests, cities and other landscapes.

The dog's sense of smell has already been extensively researched and our knowledge is based on various experiments and observations of different situations. Nevertheless, the full capability of the dog's nose's sense of smell is not well understood.

At this point I would like to quote Roger Caras, who wrote:

"The dog's nose is a wonder to us. It has remarkable characteristics and reminds us of the fact that there is a world that will never

In a world full of smells! (Photo: Mozarski)

disclose its secrets to us, at least not as long as we are human creatures."

Anatomy and function of the dog's nose

The principal function of the respiratory organ is the absorption of oxygen from the environment into the body. The respiratory apparatus starts with the outer nose and is integrated into the contour of the upper lip in domestic mammals. In humans it protrudes from the face: in domestic mammals, however, it's drawn into the facial skull and the tip of the nose only overhangs the jawline in carnivores.

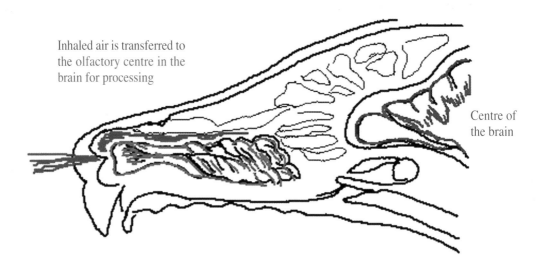

Inhaled air is transferred to
the olfactory centre in the
brain for processing

Centre of
the brain

Schematic cross-section of a dog's nose.

The respiratory system starts in the nasal cavities and continues through the pharynx, the larynx and the windpipe on to the bronchial tubes in the lungs. The inflowing air is filtered, moistened, warmed or cooled and controlled by the sense of smell at the base of the nose.

The respiratory system performs a large number of tasks. The olfactory organ in the nasal cavity controls the air. It's used for orientation in the environment and together with the rich supply of nerves, nerve fibres or impulses in the mucous membrane, it protects the dog against harmful influences from outside.

Only the dog commonly uses oral breathing – panting – mainly for evaporation of fluid. The warming of the breath is achieved by an extensive network of highly expandable and restrictable blood vessels in the mucous membrane of the nasal cavities.

A view of the dog's nose from below.
(Photo: Mozarski)

Through regular licking the dog can keep his nose
moist to a certain degree so that he can maintain opti-
mal use of his scent organ. (Photo: Mozarski)

The warmth of the blood increases the humidity in the nasal cavity, which is important for the task of smelling. Therefore it's essential to offer the dog plenty of water. Especially on very hot and dry days, the dog's mucous membrane needs a constant supply of moisture to ensure the optimum performance of the olfactory organ. The dog's nose can be affected in different ways: firstly by environmental influences such as heat, dryness and coldness, and secondly by pollution such as exhaust fumes, chemicals and other strong smells, which can hinder the dog's sense of smell.

Plant pollen, for intance oilseed rape, can affect the work, as it can constrict the nasal passages.

What is smell?

Humans distinguish fragrances from smelliness. Undoubtedly we define the sort of smell for ourselves and decide which smells are good and which are bad.

Those who are engaged in man-trailing inevitably discover a different sort of smell. They can't see, feel or smell the person but it's still almost continuously present. I am talking about the individual smell of a person.

As early as 1903 the Supreme Court of Justice of Nebraska put on record during a court case what a dog is following on a trail. In the court case Brott v. Nebraska 97 NW 593 the following is quoted:

"To get a nearer and clearer view of the nature of the evidence erroneously admitted, let us consider closely what trailing is. The path of every human being through the world, at every step, from cradle to the grave, is strewn with putrescent excretions of his body. This waste matter is in process of decomposition, it's being resolved into its constituent elements, and its power to make an impression on the olfactory nerves of the dog or other animal becomes fainter and fainter with the lapse of time."

The court of justice of Nebraska also declared that dogs are able to discriminate between smells.

"His methods of training are simple and well understood. Particles of waste matter given off fall to the ground, while undergoing chemical change come in contact with the olfactory nerves of the dog, and produce an impression which he is able to recognise, as distinct and different from all other impressions."

This quotation is so concise in its meaning that it provides a basic explanation of the term "smell".

The individual smell of a person is like an individual fingerprint that leaves its traces almost continuously. But don't confuse the individual smell with body odour. Body odour stems from poor hygiene, uncleanliness or heavy physical exercise. Body odour can be washed off or covered with other chemical smells such as deodorants.

With the individual smell this isn't possible. The source of the human smell is his body. This smell comes firstly from inside and also from the body's surface.

Factors such as inheritance, culture, environment, nutrition, emotional state, metabolism, experience and bacterial flora have an effect on it and contribute to its individuality.

Scientific studies prove that the human body consists of almost 60 billion cells. Those cells die off continuously and are replaced by new ones. Approximately 50 million cells die off every second. Specific forms of cells have different life spans:

• skin cells (epithelial cells) about 36 hours
• intestinal cells (villi cells) about 43 hours
• certain white blood cells – 13 day
• red blood cells – 120 days
• nerve cells – 100 years old

In this chapter, however, I will mainly explain the function of (epidermal) skin cells. The epidermis is the uppermost layer of the skin. The dermis (corium) is situated below. These two layers have the ability to regenerate themselves. Together they store and radiate warmth.

The human body consists of cells and is constantly giving off effluvia to the environment. The constantly dying-off cells are full of bacteria, which feed on them. The bacteria immediately start to degrade the dead skin particles as soon as they are shed, and also affect other waste material and excretions of the body. This degradation of dead tissue through bacterial influence is called decomposition, and its emerging by-products have characteristic smells that are probably a mixture of vapours and gases. Bacteria are constantly active and producing by-products.

The use of cosmetics, soaps, detergents and clothing has an additional effect. Taking drugs, drinking alcohol and smoking cigarettes can also be factors. Different conventions and diets of a culture have an effect on the individual smell.

The individual smell is also determined by the sweat, which is one of its constituent smells. Transpiration of the skin is important for heat regulation, and in turn the humidity generated is important for the existence of bacteria. It has been found that within 24 hours between 900 and 1500 millilitres of water are given off under normal circumstances. This process is continuous.

Sweat is made up of different chemical constituents, namely chloride, sodium, potassium, urea, calcium, magnesium, phosphate, sulphate, iodine, nitrate, bicarbonate, lipid, sugar and its metabolites, vitamins and hormones.

Sweat is excreted by eccrine and apocrine sweat glands, which are located at different places on the body surface. These also excrete different liquids.

Eccrine sweat glands are responsible for heat regulation, and are spread over the whole body, particularly on the forehead, the palm of the hand, the sole of the foot and in the armpit. These glands can be activated by emotional pressure or hot and spicy food.

Apocrine sweat glands are situated only in particular areas of the armpit, around the navel, at the areolae around the nipples, at the anus and around the genitals. Perspiration from these glads is caused by stress, fear or anxiety. This kind of sweat is also known as "cold sweat".

Every single one of the components mentioned makes up the scent picture of the individual. However, the development of human scent is actually more comprehensive and is only superficially dealt with in this chapter.

Skin scales
Skin scales can consist of one or several cells. According to scientific studies, the number of cells on the skin surface is said to be around

Every scent picture is so individual that the dog can retrieve the missing person with the aid of his sensitive nose.
(Photo: Lehari)

two billion. The body sheds 40 000 cells every minute.

Individual cells stick together and therefore form small and big scales. These are described as "cornflakes" because of their shape, which gives them aerodynamic qualities. Small scales are easily carried and spread by an airflow over long distances. Big scales, however, are likely to fall to the ground faster because of their weight.

The diffusion of the individual smell

Studies have proved that there is an airflow next to the skin's surface that is warmer than the air in the environment. This airflow starts at the feet and travels up to the head, wearing off at about 40 centimetres above the head. When the outside temperature goes down, the speed of the airflow increases. Clothes do not impede these airflows, in fact, they can increase their speed. By undoing a done-up garments the confined air can escape.

The dead skin particles that the body has shed are carried away to the environment with the airflow. A trail is left by the decomposition of the bacteria and the released cloud of gas. Lightweight particles float in the air a longer before they fall to the ground than heavier ones. Outside temperature and air humidity have an effect on decomposition.

Interference by environmental factors

Environmental factors also have a significant effect and determine how long the trail is available to the dog. There are climatic factors, such as temperature, light and air and ground humidity, but also wind, radiation, fire and ground motion.

⮩ Wind and wind speed

There are different wind conditions in the air and close to the ground. Also, turbulence can occur due to differences in temperature. The skin particles, with the bacteria and the "cloud of scent", are carried away and spread by the wind, sometimes over great distances. The heavier skin scales fall to the ground quicker and closer to their origin than the lighter ones. Before landing, they meet ground turbulence, which can be generated through grass, vegetation and swirling.

⮩ Temperature

Temperatures have a direct influence on bacterial activity. Through extremely high or low temperatures their growth rate is considerably reduced or even stopped completely. The optimum temperature for bacterial growth is 37 degrees Celsius. Temperature varies, as does wind speed, with the distance from the ground.

⮩ Humidity

Humidity is essential for the growth of bacteria. Hot and dry air deprives the bacteria of nourishing humidity until they stop working. Skin particles or, rather, skin scales that land on hot ground start to dry up.

The formation of dew in the evening or in the early morning supplies the cells with water. This enables the surviving bacteria to continue the decomposition and to multiply. The reproductive process of bacteria is very short. The smell produced is thought to be stronger when decomposition is resumed than when the ground is hot and dry.

The activity of the bacteria changes throughout the day. Skin scales that fall to the ground on a hot afternoon might be easier to locate in the evening. Because of the formation of dew and the lower temperatures, the activity is strongest at that point. In contrast, the processing of the scales that accumulated overnight stagnates. As soon as morning dew is formed the bacteria get active again and reach an optimum of olfactory development with the increase in temperature. Therefore the trail is

This dog is searching for the scent along the edge of the bushes. (Photo: Mozarski)

Here the dog is following the trail along the kerb of a street. (Photo: Mozarski)

supposed to be most easily perceived by the dog in the morning.

➲ Rain

The trail is reinforced through light rain. Strong ongoing rain, however, will wash away the skin scales because of their oily and gaseous consistency. This can result in an interruption of the trail.

➲ Sunlight

Sunlight also influences bacteria. Ultraviolet, violet and blue rays have an anti-bacterial effect. Green, red and yellow rays have less effect.

➲ Time factor

Bacterial decomposition starts with the shedding of the skin particles. This is accompanied by the development of smell, which can vary in intensity. There are many environmental factors and influences that have an effect on the development of smell.

Because of unlimited potential variations it's not possible to determine and predict how long a trail is preserved.

Development and diffusion of the trail

When a person is moving, skin scales, with their cloud of scent, float in the air for some time. While they are floating they are referred to as "scent in the air". Other, heavier scales, in contrast, fall to the ground quicker. Those form the actual trail.

When and where the scales finally accumulate is firstly down to the environmental influences I mentioned. Secondly, the ground surface plays a role. Areas covered with vegetation keep the scales well grounded. Bushes can form a barrier. Bare areas such as asphalt, concrete or rock hardly form a barrier, so the scales can spread farther to some extent until they are stopped by an obstacle.

All these criteria have to be taken into account when working. This is why it's essential to train at different times of the day. Different environmental conditions during the day can influence the dog. Every dog has its individual upper limit. However, you shouldn't presume that the dog can only follow a trail under ideal circumstances. It lies with you to find out where the limits of your team are.

In this chapter I can only explain basically what smell is and how it acts under outside influences. It's therefore advisable to acquire further knowledge on the subject of scent and the dog's smelling abilities.

In addition to the basic theory, personal experience and reports from other man-trailing teams will be very valuable.

The search along the fence leads back to the house wall. (Photo: Lehari)

Training preparations

The equipment required

Good suitable equipment is required for any kind of training and any operation. This should be practical and easy to handle. The dog handler's clothing or uniform should be functional and comfortable. The dog's equip-ment needs to be well fitting and hard-wearing. Nothing should hinder or hurt the team while working.

The dog's harness
The harness should be made of robust material. Leather, of course, is a popular material. How-

ever, there are also harnesses made of nylon, which are also suitable for beginners.

The important thing is that the harness is well fitted to the dog. Strain shouldn't be applied on the dog's neck but on the chest. In order that the fit is right, the dog's neck and chest girth should be measured before purchase.

Make sure that the harness isn't too big; otherwise it could cause friction injuries. The material shouldn't be too hard or have overlapping hems or double-stitching.

The variety available is extensive, so you should find the right harness for your dog.

Chalk-markings on the asphalt. (Photo: Mozarski)

On fields or in the forests the trail can be easily indicated with these little flags. (Photo: Mozarski)

The trailing lead

Here, mainly, the same rules apply as for the harness . A lead made of soft leather, of course, is the best choice and most comfortable for the dog handler's hands. In the beginning, certainly, a lead made of nylon is fine, too, although the possibility of burns should be considered when the lead slips through the fingers. It's therefore advisable to wear light gloves.

For training in the woods and on fields a 10 metre lead is recommended. For trails in the city 5 metre leads are more practical.

Don't forget to take the dog's everyday collar and lead with you, as he needs to change after trailing.

Indications

Training takes place in different surroundings with different ground conditions, so the trails are indicated accordingly. There are several possibilities for this purpose:

• chalk on asphalt
• little flags in the woods and on fields
• ribbons
• spray chalk

On long trails it's important to offer the dog water regularly. (Photo: Lehari)

Even a water fountain can satisfy the thirst, as with this bloodhound. (Photo: Freier)

Plastic bags for scent articles

In order to be able to transport and preserve scent articles, you will need plastic bags in different sizes. Clear or white resealable freezer bags are most suitable. Brown or green rubbish bags are inadvisable as they are often perfumed and therefore can influence the scent article.

Water bottle for the dog

When the dog's equipment is purchased you also need to arrange for his physical well-being. The trail is exhausting for him, so you should never forget his water bottle. It depends on the length of the trail and the temperature how much water the dog should be offered in between and after work. On very long trails the dog will probably also need water while working.

Jackpot for the dog

At the end of the trail the dog needs to be rewarded and acknowledged accordingly. When picking out jackpots you need to find out for yourself what your dog likes. The important thing is that it's something special for your dog – sausages or cheese cut into small pieces or something similar, perhaps. Many dogs also appreciate a good game with a ball at the end of the trail (also see "Reward after work").

Safety equipment for handler and dog

Dress in an eye-catching way so that you are visible even from far away, especially in traffic. High-visibility vests or coats are best. They should have reflective tape on so that you are clearly visible, even in the dark.

The dog should also be identified clearly as a working dog and wear a High-visibility safety coat.

Other useful items

Working a trail can be stressful enough in itself, so you shouldn't carry unnecessary ballast with you. A bum bag or a small backpack to stow away the equipment is useful. So as to avoid offending others if the dog "leaves something behind", take plenty of bags for cleaning up after him.

Well-fitting security clothing is important for the handler so that he is clearly visible, even from far away and in the dark. (Photo: Lehari)

There are safety coats with "cat's eyes" for dogs too. (Photo: Mozarski)

Equipment required for training.
(Photo: Lehari)

Everything packed?

Here is a short checklist:
• harness
• trailing lead
• collar and lead
• plastic bag for scent articles
• water bottle for the dog
• reward for the dog
• plastic bag to remove droppings
• small first-aid kit
• compass
• pen and paper
• latex gloves
• walkie-talkie or mobile phone
• high-visibility jacket

A small first-aid kit is always advisable in case the dog, or even the handler, gets hurt.

A compass and a torch help with orientation. A head torch will allow you to have both hands free. You should also carry some paper and a pen with you in case you need to write some keywords down. Latex gloves are useful when handling the scent article or other objects at the site.

Walkie-talkies or a mobile phone are essential in man-trailing. The handler always needs to be accessible. Exchange of information of any kind is extremely important.

Scent articles

Every object the missing person has had contact with is called a scent article. These include all materials the person has for instance touched, carried or worn as clothing.

The human smell sticks to all those things and is therefore presented to the dog as a scent article to enable him to find the matching trail and follow it. The scent article can be the key to success but also to failure. You should therefore make it a rule to treat it very carefully and to respect the following rules.

An assortment of potential scent articles. (Photo: Lehari)

The stronger the smell of the scent article, the greater the chance that the dog will filter it out and follow the right track. This is especially important for beginners or young dogs, as we want to keep it as simple as possible for them in the beginning. Clothes worn by the missing person are ideal.

Scent articles can be varied as you wish. Try jackets, shirts, T-shirts, pyjamas, underwear and socks, for instance, but also pillows, car seats, hairbrushes, toothbrushes,and so on. Then there are objects the person has touched or encountered, for example, wallets, keys, cig-arette ends, cigarette packets, discarded chewing gum, door handles and so on. Some objects are better than others and these increase your chances of success.

Basically, scent particles stick better to rough material than to smooth.

So, for instance, pyjamas worn all night are more heavily tainted with scent particles than the door handle that was only briefly touched.

The human individual smell is especially distinctive in all body fluids. Blood, sweat, used tissues, soiled nappies, urine, saliva or vomit make very good scent articles.

Experiment as much as possible and write down the results in your training records. Give your imagination free rein when choosing scent articles.

Depending on the situation on the site, it could be necessary to make a scent article yourself. This is required when there is only one scent article available. It's even possible that there is no scent article of the missing person available, but only an object that he has been in contact with. This might be a car seat, chair, windowsill, windowpane, steering wheel or something else.

With a piece of sterile muslin the smell can be picked up from a car seat, chair or steering wheel. The muslin should be in direct contact with the particular object for about 10 to 15 minutes and then be stored in a firmly closed plastic bag for at least 10 minutes.

This method will give you suitable scent articles that can also be kept for further use.

Correct handling of the scent article

It's crucial that the scent article is handled correctly and well protected and packed. Therefore the scent article is put into a plastic bag and sealed. The scent lingers in the bag and is presented to the dog before starting. Make sure that nobody else has touched or carried the scent article before. Careless handling could be the decisive factor in an unsuccessful start or failure on a trail.

Contaminated or difficult scent articles and poor-quality scent articles are used during training, too, but this is under controlled conditions designed to teach the handler how his dog reacts under such circumstances.

On a mission it's important that the dog handler packs the scent article himself. Check the available articles and decide which one will allow your dog the best evaluation of the scent. If possible, articles covered with other smells should be avoided. From time to time another person may have touched the scent article. This can't always be prevented. This person is then presented to the dog to be sniffed at before the trail so that the dog can associate the smell with the particular person and exclude it from the search.

Don't let yourself be misled or put under pressure. The dog handler is the one who chooses the scent article and packs it. This allows the dog the best chance to finish the trail successfully.

Ideally, shoes shouldn't be used. Many contain synthetic materials that also have a strong characteristic smell, which could mask the individual smell.

On a mission it sometimes happens that only the missing person's worn shoes are available. In this case, make sure that the dog picks up the scent from inside the shoe. Work on this situation once your dog is confident in picking up smells.

When a piece of cloth to be used as a scent article has been in contact with other smells (for instance, the laundry basket), it's turned inside out to bring out the individual scent.

With caps and hats the dog should sniff the inside, as this is where the person had direct body contact.

The correct, careful handling of the scent article is important. Young dogs or beginners get only one piece of cloth to pick up the smell at first. When the dog has understood this you can start to vary different scent articles.

The trail-layer and his job

An "actual"missing person must belong to every scent article. This is very important for the whole training process, as without a trail the training can't take place.

During basic training it's important that the dog reaches the destination with high motivation. Therefore we let our helper run away with exact training instructions. The trail-layer, as well as the man-trailer himself, should be familiar with the whole subject of man-trailing. Otherwise, it's your job to instruct the helper correctly.

Before each training session the programme is discussed and the trail-layer is responsible for sticking to the agreements. Walkie-talkies are a great help in avoiding mistakes.

Important!
Man-trailer and trail-layer discuss the training process in detail and the trail-layer sticks to the course of the trail discussed. This means that a right-hand bend remains exactly that, and is to be performed as such.

The role of the trail-layer is very important. He is the linchpin of the whole training. The following example illustrates this.

The man-trailer and the trail-layer have agreed on a certain trail. The trail-layer doesn't stick to this path and opts for a different direction. The man-trailer now corrects his dog into a direction that the missing person has not taken. Through this wrong correction the dog learns to follow a "ghost trail". He thinks that his owner smells the right way better than he does and will always wait for a sign from his handler in the future.

Therefore try to involve as many family members and friends as possible so that you always have enough people "disappear" and can work with a variety of "victims".

Indications
Dog handler and trail-layer have to speak the same language. If trails are indicated, both need to know the meaning of the marks. The training trail can be indicated differently.

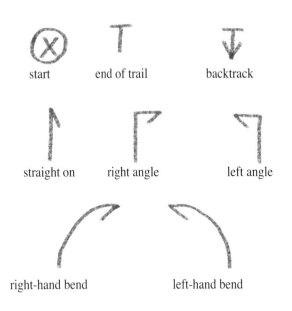

start   end of trail   backtrack

straight on   right angle   left angle

right-hand bend   left-hand bend

Chalk indications and their meanings.

Depending on how the flags are positioned they have a different meaning.

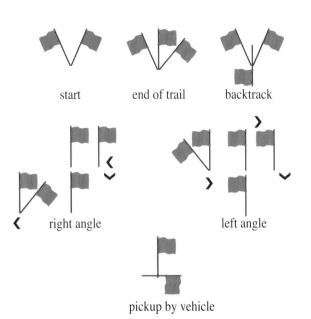

start   end of trail   backtrack

right angle   left angle

pickup by vehicle

In the city it's wise to work with chalk indications ideally using standardized marks.

In the forest and on fields little flags are used to indicate particular directions and illustrate symbols.

Helpers and companions

On a mission it's essential to have an experienced helper with you when working a trail. He knows the dog's body language and working style just as well as his handler does. The helper isn't there for entertainment but to take on important jobs and support the handler. He should be in a position about 5 metres behind the man-trailing team. From there he can follow and observe the working dog clearly and unhampered. From that perspective the helper has a good overview and can sometimes observe the dog better than the handler himself. When searching in the city the helper can keep an eye on the traffic ahead and manage it if necessary. The helper should always make sure that he doesn't hinder the dog and the handler while working. In addition he is much valued water and for carrying other items.

But the helper's support is also important in training. In team-training he is the one who knows the course of the trail, who observes the man-trailing team and provides support.

Training documentation

Every new area that we enter requires a solid basic education with continual development. The diversity required in man-trailing can only be implemented with a well-organized training plan. For various reasons it's therefore useful to document the whole training process in detail.

By constantly writing down the different training trails, every single step can be reconstructed and the dog's progress can be monitored. This allows you to discover where problems arise and which fields of activity need further intensive training.

All possible situations and conditions have to be taken into account during training, such as the age of the trail, the type of surroundings, weather conditions, contamination, time of day and so on. The training notes also serve as a qualification for the man-trailing team, which some organizations demand as a certificate. So spend time documenting the entire training in detail.

The helper should always keep a certain distance from the man-trailing team. (Photo: Lehari)

Dog handler	Dog	Date

Position	Length	Terrain

trail runner 1 – scent article trail runner 1 – scent article	trail runner 2 – scent article trail runner 2 – scent article

laying of the track	start of the search	person(s) found
date	date	date
time	time	time
☐ morning ☐ afternoon ☐ evening/night	☐ morning ☐ afternoon ☐ evening/night	☐ morning ☐ afternoon ☐ evening/night

environmental conditions

temperature	wind	conditions
when laying: °C	☐ windless ☐ breezy ☐ unsettled ☐ steady ☐ squally ☐ stormy	☐ clear ☐ partly cloudy ☐ cloudy ☐ light rain ☐ strong rain ☐ fog

environmental conditions

temperature	wind	conditions
when laying: °C	☐ windless ☐ breezy ☐ unsettled ☐ steady ☐ squally ☐ stormy	☐ clear ☐ partly cloudy ☐ cloudy ☐ light rain ☐ strong rain ☐ fog

training area:

description of the trail – course and speed

particularities – comments

Handling of the lead

The lead is the nerve that connects dog and handler. It transmits information to the handler that tells him what his dog is finding out on the trail.

So the handling and control of the lead is an extra skill that should be trained without a dog first. Practise dry runs with a human partner with each of you taking turns as dog and then handler. Run through different gaits – slow walking, changing to running, sudden stops, zigzag, and so on – basically as your dog will do.

It's important not to hinder the dog. Constant jerky movements of the lead can confuse him and make him insecure. Some dogs understand the jerk as a correction and leave the trail.

The lead should have light tension during the whole trail without hindering the dog. He shouldn't feel traction. It must be pointed out that the lead needs to be reeled in, followed up and rolled up in the hand when the dog reduces his speed or stops. When the dog starts moving again we let the lead slip through our fingers and give him the working radius he needs, while maintaining constant light tension.

When your dog has to go round obstacles such as trees, posts, poles or the like, the lead is passed into one hand as, the other hand reaches around the object and picks up the lead without disturbing the dog.

How the lead is held correctly. (Photo: Freier)

Before starting training you should practise some "dry runs" at handling the lead. (Photo: Freier)

Stop your dog on the track deliberately, as this is also a typical situation. It's often necessary to stop the dog because of traffic or to take a drinking break.

When doing dry runs with a human partner you will quickly realize how your dog must feel in real life when he continually gets impulses through false handling of the lead. Therefore the lead is under constant light tension and is reeled in and then unreeled.

The dog handler must choose the length of the lead for himself, depending on the terrain.

In the city it's important to keep the lead as short as possible for safety reasons. It must be pointed out that every dog has his own limits, which determine whether he is comfortable or uncomfortable. You will find the correct distance between dog and handler for yourself. Above all, the dog shouldn't be hindered.

In open areas or forests the distance between do handler and dog can be enlarged. Train all lead distances to avoid any problems. A good lead technique will help you learn to

When trailing, the dog is allowed to pull on the lead heavily and has to pull his partner along in the same direction. (Photo: Mozarski)

read the dog. By and by the team becomes harmonious and more reliable.

The pre-scent

The term "pre-scent" has not been utilized in man-trailing language use so far. In order to avoid repetition, the term is introduced at this point and its meaning is explained below scent.

Putting the scent article on the ground in front of the dog before getting the harness on is a very effective and useful technique. When the scent article is packed into a plastic bag, open the bag and pull down the sides

As soon as the dog has picked up the scent from the plastic bag he indicates that he is ready to follow the trail. (Photos: Lehari)

so that the scent article lies in front of the dog. This allows him enough time to pick up the smell of the scent article in front of him while the harness is put on. My own experiences have shown that the dog has already familiarized himself with the smell and and determined the direction of the missing person before I even give the starting command. He then indicates the direction with the posture of his head and his glance.

In the majority of cases the plastic bag with the scent article is positioned right in front of the dog's nose once again after the harness is put on. Many dogs pick up the scent thoroughly by sticking their nose into the plastic bag and then indicate quite quickly that they have already picked up the right trail.

The start is a crucial part on every successful trail. The dog's motivation, the presentation of the scent article and the uptake of the smell, as well as the location of the trail, are vital here. Everything needs to be coordinated so that the dog can do a good job. Nothing is worse than a spoilt start.

The start is always performed steadily and above all with calm and confident handling. The harness can be the cue for the dog that prepares him for a trail. I have found a regular ritual has proved valuable. You should carefully commit every single hand movement and the order to memory. Consistency strengthens the process and gives you and your dog the necessary confidence.

The start

You are about to start. You arrive for training and get a dog out of the car. It's important to let the dog be a dog before training. He should have the freedom to do his business and to get acquainted with his new environment and its smells. Offer him the opportunity to explore the new territory and to go to the toilet.

When the dog has dealt with the surroundings visually and, more importantly, with the existing smells, he won't be so distracted later when you start training and he will be able to concentrate on his job better.

The dog handler takes the harness and the lead out of the car, not forgetting the reward and the dog's water bottle. Everything is prepared calmly so that there are no unnecessary delays and confusion for the dog later on at the start. This means that the lead is untangled so that it can be attached to the harness readily.

The dog's harness should be put on in a calm and quick manner and only when the dog is ready for the trail. In this way the dog is tuned into trailing with your voice, which promises him that something really good is about to happen.

When putting on the harness one option is to have the dog between your straddled legs. The purpose of this is that you can restrain him gently with your legs to prevent him jumping around. This shouldn't happen with force, as you don't want to make the dog feel worried. The other option is to go down on your knees to the dog and put on the harness calmly then. It depends on the dog which option is best and you simply have to try it out.

Don't be too ambitious in the beginning. The dog shouldn't be pushed into position by giving him the "sit" command or even by pulling or jerking the lead. If you apply pressure, man-trailing work could have a negative effect on the dog. Let your dog howl with enthusiasm and joy as you are about to start.

When the dog is standing between your legs, which should be leaning slightly against his hips and ribs, you can influence him without throwing commands at him. Furthermore, this leaves both hands free to put on the dog's harness and present the scent article.

The dog should learn that man-trailing is a kind of hunt that is fun for him. This is the only way to make the dog perform this task with you eagerly again and again.

The starting command

So what do I say at the beginning of the trail, and when do I say it exactly? Timing of the presentation of the scent article and the command "Find" is very important. The dog must associate the command unmistakably with the scent article and pick up its trail scent and follow it.

How the harness is put on. (Photo: Lehari)

If your four-legged partner has something else on his mind, don't give the starting command. There is a great danger of the dog being more interested in the cat he has just seen than

Picking on the harness. (Photo: Lehari)

Picking up the scent. (Photo: Lehari)

in the human track we have presented him with.

During the first training session the trail-layer entices the dog with the jackpot and runs away from him. This stimulates the dog's natural instinct for following fugitives. In this case it's finding the missing person. The scent article needs to be associated with a command by the trail-layer. Use a word that is short and concise. I use the word

"Find". From the moment when the scent article is presented to the dog this one command is now used. That means that the dog handler gives the command once at the start and doesn't repeat it during the rest of the trail.

You can use other words such as, for instance, "Where is he?", "Show me" or "Search him", to encourage the dog to work later on in the trail.

Start. (Photo: Lehari)

The starting command is a clear, monosyllabic word such as, "Find", which should be associated with the presentation of the scent article.

Motivate the dog at the start with your voice.

Command language

As always, you need to find a happy medium to motivate and reward the dog at the start and on the trail. Through volume, length or shortness, acuity and strictness of the commands the dog understands what you mean. Find the right tone. Not saying anything and walking silently behind the dog isn't motivating. But talking at the dog constantly can be equally bad.

Stopping on the trail, such as, at the roadside, must be practised with the dog. (Photo: Lehari)

A happy, calm command such as "Where is he?" can work wonders on a longer trail. With experience and by observing the effect of your voice on the dog you can improve your success rate.

Constant talking to the dog in a sharp tone will quickly make him switch off. It's necessary and sometimes even mandatory to stop the dog on the trail because roads have to be crossed or the dog needs a drinking break. In this case the commands "Halt" or "Stop" can be used.

Train your dog in stopping on the trail, as at the next street crossing the traffic lights may be on red. To do this, keep the lead short and bring the dog to a stop with a command

The jackpot will always motivate the dog to start a new search all over again. (Foto: Lehari)

such as, "Good dog", given in a calm and friendly tone.

Reward after work

Nothing is free – and this is why even a dog wants to be "paid" for his job after his work is done. The dog should choose his reward himself. It's your job to find out what stimulates the individual dog so much that it's his "bee's knees". The jackpot can be food or a toy, but it should be more than just verbal praise.

"Celebrate" your dog after each training session and reward him so that he is happy and enthusiastic enough to perform the task again and again, eagerly and with drive. Your exuberant tone lets the dog know that he has done a really good job, and he will be very happy that his two-legged partner is so delighted with him. Go down on your knees so that you are on the same level as your dog.

The second reward then can be a game with his ball or a squeaky toy. Some dogs prefer something really special to eat. And I don't mean boring dry food here. One dog would do anything for a piece of cheese; another loves sausages; cooked pork liver is said to have worked wonders with others. Baileys, a Labrador bitch, for example, is "celebrated" with lots of fun and praise after each training session and then gets her favourite toy, a ball.

Important!
It's only through the sufficient reward at the end of the trail that the dog will stay on the course of the trail and won't be distracted from the track by other stimulat smells.

It's just so nice to see how happy she is and how she tells we humans with grunting noises and her whole body language: "Did you see how amazing I am and what I did?"

Only if the dog gets a sufficient reward at the end of the trail will he start the next trail with drive in order to earn his reward. Of course, an experienced dog won't stop working immediately if he isn't rewarded sufficiently now and then. But over a certain period of time an insufficient reward will lessen his motivation.

Our exuberant verbal and physical praise ought to stimulate the dog's desire to have the great reward. Even if some dogs don't seem to care about our praise and are only interested in getting their reward we mustn't start to contain our applause. Our mood will be transmitted to the dog, although he is focused on the reward.

If you use the dog's harness as a key cue at the end and the beginning of the trail, it's removed shortly after the verbal praise and before the delivery of the reward. If the dog is rewarded with a toy, he is rewarded verbally or with a treat first after finding the missing person. Then he is released from the harness and can concentrate on playing with his toy.

The dog will only work with high motivation when searching pays off for him!

When the dog has worked a trail well and has been "celebrated" and rewarded accordingly he is brought back into the car immediately. Now he can quietly think about what he has learned beforehand and what a successful hunt it was.

Identification

The dog has worked the course of a trail and has reached the destination. He has found the

An indication by jumping up on the person is a dog's natural behaviour. The dog knows that he is now praised enthusiastically and gets the jackpot.

The jumping up may have been generated by the runner holding the jackpot in front of her body at waist height during training. In order to get to his reward the dog jumped up on the person. Therefore you should consider the dog's size and decide whether it's appropriate to let him jump up on this person.

Some dogs can also indicate by sitting in front of the located person. During training, as soon as the dog sits in front of the person he is generously rewarded by them. The person can also ask the dog to sit and then reward him with his jackpot.

It's up to the dog handler to decide on the form of indication. Observe your dog and encourage his natural tendency. The same method of indication should then be adopted every time.

The located person can be indicated by the dog sitting in front of her. (Photo: Lehari)

missing person. Now it's his job to identify and indicate the person accordingly. The form of indication can vary. Some dogs jump up on a standing person or sit in front of her. Others indicate by barking at the person.

Training on an indicated trail

Dog training is the first part of the training. The dog handler knows the course of the trail, or the trail is indicated accordingly for him, for instance, with chalk symbols. The purpose is to be able to read and understand the dog correctly on the trail and to be able to observe him in certain situations. Whether new situations are being integrated into the trail or the whole trail is being trained, the dog handler has the opportunity to observe his dog and to discover how he works and when he has difficulties in working a trail. An indicated trail allows him to study the dog's body language and his reactions freely without other concerns. By observing the dog on a known trail the dog handler can learn about the dog's negative indications and find out whether the dog corrects himself on a crossing trail or at the end of the trail.

It's important that we don't influence or affect the dog while he is working on the trail. The dog handler should always be positioned behind the dog. When the course of the trail is known you tend to walk quickly alongside the dog or even to overtake him. That way the dog is guided along the trail, which doesn't make sense.

Be careful not to give the dog the feeling that you know better or that you can smell better than him. Dogs quickly understand when their handler knows the way.

Even through small signs such as, for instance, an overhasty turn of the shoulder into the desired direction the dog is given unconscious help. The result will be a dog that keeps looking for his handler and waits to be helped. The dog needs to have the feeling of going home as the winner. He has followed the trail and found the person.

The dog handler needs to be able to interpret the dog's behaviour correctly and he must not influence the dog in any way. (Photo: Lehari)

Reading the dog on the trail is one of the most important requirements for a successful team.

You will acquire this ability in time with all the experiences that you accrue during the whole training process. Reading and interpreting the dog correctly can lead a search to success.

The dog handler needs to know how the dog behaves when he has lost the track or missed the direction.

The correct interpretation of the dog's body language in different training situations can be crucial for a later mission. The dog handler studies his dog – the dog is the winner of the trail!

Every handler needs to develop a feeling for not guiding his dog along the course of indicated or known trails.

I know from experience that often the question comes up whether the dog follows the chalk symbols and learns to reach the destination by somehow using them as signposts. The following practical example is useful.

We were training in a residential area with chalk indications. Children who were playing in the streets had also painted arrows, lines or the like on the pavement with chalk. My dog now had a whole range of chalk symbols on the way that he perceived as well as I did. However, he didn't follow the children's signs.

Dogs that have learned to follow an individual smell naturally pick up what we as quarries leave or lose on the trail. The dog needs to have the opportunity to investigate those things to find out whether they match the missing person.

Here it's useful to ask the trail-layer to lose objects on the trail. This could be tissues, sweet wrappers or other things. He should scrabble with his feet in the forest or on other soft ground. He can even sit down on a bench in between. When your dog accepts these objects and signposts you should praise him, as he has smelt that the person has been there and lost objects. This improves his motivation.

You can also replace the indications with marking tape or ribbons. Attach these in a position so that the dog can't see the indications.

Where you still doubt whether the dog is following the trail correctly you should check his performance immediately. Ask the runner to run a known trail for you without indications. Another person accompanies him and indicates the trail with chalk symbols. Shortly before the end of the trail this person takes another route. What does the dog do? Does he follow the trail that isn't indicated? If he isn't doing that and follows the indications there has been a training error, which is that the dog has not yet associated the scent article with the missing person.

The team should be working the trail together, so the helper isn't allowed to give away the course of the trail. (Photo: Lehari)

Team training on a non-indicated trail

The second important part of the training is team training. In this case the dog handler doesn't know the course of the trail. The handler needs to rely on his knowledge and experience and needs to trust his dog completely. Another helper is needed who knows the course of the trail or who has laid out the quarry. This person walks with the dog and the handler and can – if necessary – offer the handler appropriate support during the search. The helper can help in difficult situations and contribute to a successful retrieve.

It's important that the helper only steps in when the handler and dog are dissipating their energies completely or are walking in the wrong direction.

In this situation the timing of the helper's support is very important. The dog handler needs to learn what the dog will do when he can't relocate the smell he should follow, or when he walks in another direction. How does the handler deal with a dog that suddenly stops the search or circles around enquiringly?

The aim is that dog handler and dog help one another and work the trail together. If the dog indicates something negative the handler must be able to recognize the situation and to react and interfere accordingly.

The helper should only provide guidance and never give away the course of the trail because otherwise team training turns into dog training.

Team training is training for the dog handler and the dog on an unknown trail. Trust your dog unless you can smell better than him!

Basic trail

The basic trail is the cornerstone of all man-trailing work. The exercise is carried out as described here. One person entices the dog with the jackpot and a scent article, then calls the dog's name. The dog is already harnessed. The dog handler also "heats up" his dog. The dog's interest in the person is aroused. The person then drops the scent article and runs away from the dog.

The running away is supported by verbal sounds such as, for instance, "Hey, hey, hey". The runner races a straight line and positions himself at the end so that the dog can see him. The dog handler guides his dog to the scent article. As soon as he sniffs the article the command "Find" is given and the dog is allowed to go and follow the person. When he has found her he is rewarded generously, which increases the dog's motivation enormously. The fun factor comes first.

Don't make it harder and more complicated for the dog than it is. Difficult tasks and working out new situations can be built up with the basic trail. Therefore it's not necessary to run mile-long trails in the beginning. The focus is on working the trail and on coping with an unknown situation quickly and successfully.

Combine a task with the basic trail and let your dog perform the task. When he has understood and associated this you can incorporate this new task into the trail at another place.

Here is a useful example. A car seat serves as scent article. Let your dog observe the person getting up from the seat and walking away

Set-up of a basic trail. (Photos: Mozarski)

from the car. As soon as the person is out of sight put the dog on the trail at the car seat and start him. A trail length of about 50 metres is enough.

From my own experience I can say never underestimate the basic trail. Follow every successful trail the dog completes with a basic trail. This will maintain and increase the dog's motivation.

A dog handler should always keep the following in mind a dog can only be a successful man-trailer if he has sufficient motivation and enjoys the work. The basic trail is the cornerstone for a whole man-trailing career.

Training programme

Training structure basics

A training programme must be well developed and structured. It should create a stable foundation for the dog handler and his dog. Therefore always make sure not to run before you can walk. Be satisfied with little progress. Your expectations shouldn't be too high. Develop a ritual for the course of your search. This ritual should be followed so that the dog knows what to expect.

Only through a solid, consistent training structure that a man-trailing team can grow and mature.

When a puppy is being trained for man-trailing work you can let him run together with older and more experienced dogs. Dogs are pack animals. They instinctively look to the older pack members for guidance and knowledge.

Absolute beginners

This stage is for dogs that have never followed a trail before. The dog's age is irrelevant. You should start with the basic trail (explained in the previous chapter) no matter whether the dog has trailing experience or has no idea what to expect. The dog needs to associate the scent article with the corresponding person first.

To begin with, you should keep in mind the following and integrate it into your training.

The runner should be familiar with the dog. Otherwise both should have the time to "sniff" at each other first. The dog's interest in the person is sparked by a good play and feeding treats before starting.

Training should take place on a mown meadow, in a park, on a field path or in the woods. Choose an environment with as few people as possible. The runner races against the wind! He thus runs into the wind so that the smell is carried back to the dog.

The dog is enticed with treats and the scent article.
(Photos: Mozarski)

Structure and sequence of a basic trail. (Photos: Mozarski)

Exercise 1

The dog is already harnessed. The runner entices him verbally as well as with treats and the scent article. Use a large scent article such as a jacket or a T-shirt. The runner then drops the scent article and runs away. The dog observes the runner, who keeps enticing him verbally while running away from him. The course should follow a straight line of about 30 to 50 metres length. At the end of the trail the runner positions himself so as to be clearly visible to the dog. The dog handler now guides his dog to the scent article. As soon as the dog puts his nose down to the scent article the handler gives a command such as "Find". Most dogs then run straight up to the person. Arriving there, the dog is "celebrated" and generously rewarded.

You can build additional help for the dog into the basic trail. The runner can drag off a scent article when running away. Attach another worn T-shirt to a rope. By dragging the second scent article the runner puts additional smell on the course.

If the dog isn't interested in the scent article at first you can spark his interest with a treat. The runner visibly puts a treat, such as, a piece of sausage, onto the scent article. As soon as the dog picks it up the starting command is given. Give this command once only. You can continue to motivate the dog to search with other words such as "Where is he."

The dog should have enough lead length during this exercise. Let him run freely. Should the

The dog's nose is inside the scent article. (Photo: Mozarski)

dog stop or seem to be confused for some reason, ask the runner to motivate the dog to come to him by calling his name again.

Puppies or older dogs that need additional motivation can be launched immediately while the runner is still racing.

This triggers the instinct to follow moving objects. Motivation and generous rewarding at the end of the trail are very important for the dog. This is how he realizes that he has done something good and will be highly motivated again for the next trail.

During the stage of training where the dog is verbally and physically enticed by the runner the dog is already harnessed.

Exercise 2

The task is the same as for exercise 1. The difference is simply that the runner goes with the wind.

Exercise 3

The starting position is the same as for exercise 1. The runner first races on a straight line and then adds an angle or a curve. This can be a hiding place behind a tree, a bush or a house. The dog at first observes the runner who then disappears from view.

Exercise 4

The dog observes the runner walking away. Then the dog is walked around so that he doesn't see the runner anymore. You can, for example, go behind a car with your dog. As soon as the runner is out of sight the dog is guided to the scent article. At the starting command he takes off. With this exercise it's important to change the dog's starting direction. Put him on the track diagonally, for instance, or even in the opposite direction to the trail course.

These exercises are trained at different places again and again. Change to places with

The person walks on a straight line and then makes a turn. The dog needs to follow the trail, as he can't see the person anymore. (Photo: Mozarski)

a few more people, although obviously not a crowded shopping street. Change from forests to field and meadows to train the passage from forest soil to field soil, or start on a meadow and switch back to the forest. Try switching from gravel paths or meadows to asphalt.

Practise many different surface and environment changes. Your runner shouldn't only

pass field or forest paths. He should leave small paths and continue walking across a field or through the forest. Thereby the dog learns that a path isn't automatically a trail.

With different training environments the training conditions will vary too. On an open field you usually have different wind conditions from those found in a hedged forest. This must be taken into account in your training plan.

The dog is further motivated when he finds other objects belonging to the missing person. The runner should – as already mentioned – lose a tissue or a sweet wrapper on the trail. He should also touch objects. For this he sits down on a bench or a tree trunk.

An example of the course of a trail. (Photos: Lehari)

In addition he could scratch on the ground with his shoes and leave a mark.

The dog is reassured by this additional information that the person has stopped in those places. This motivates him to continue following the smell.

The training result should be that the dog has learned to associate the scent article with the corresponding person. When the dog shows you that he has understood this task you can begin to increase and vary the requirements.

*The dog needs to learn the association
between the scent article and the missing
person. (Photo: Mozarski)*

The distance is gradually increased up to 90
metres. Additional turns and curves are integrated. The time span between the disappearance of the runner and the start is also
increased. Wait up to 10 to 15 minutes before
starting your dog.

Longer distances should be indicated by the runner. This allows you to observe your dog on the trail. If your dog takes another way or departs too far from the trail just stand still and wait until he returns to the actual course of the trail and continues following it.

Be careful not to freeze when stopping. Keep moving in slightly rhythmic motions. As soon as the dog has recovered the trail, praise him.

Beginners

Exercise

The runner has already laid an indicated trail of 50 to 90 metres and is out of the dog's sight. He has left a scent article at the starting point. The trail itself should include three or four turns or curves. The dog, which has not seen the person before, is now prepared for the trail. Remember to let him explore the environment first. Then put the dog on the trail in the previously described order of prescenting – harnessing – start.

Beginners are usually not allowed to depart too far from the trail. Allow your dog a lead length of about 4 metres. The dog should move no farther from the course of the trail. If he does so, however, stand still until he is on the trail again and keeps following it. As soon as he resumes work and follows the course of the trail, praise him in the correct tone.

If the dog should have serious difficulties you can ask the runner to come back into the dog's sight. The runner should then leave his hiding place and approach the dog. This technique helps the dog without restricting him.

After successfully completing this trail, add a short basic trail. Let the person run away again for about 4 or 5 metres and send your dog straight away. Again the dog is enthusiastically praised and "celebrated".

Further exercises

Gradually increase the time span between the laying of the trail by the runner and the start of the search up to between 30 and 60 minutes. Increase the length of the trail up to 400 metres.

Only if your dog has understood these tasks and has no serious problems with the search can you prepare the next step. Now you introduce street crossings, starting with narrow footpaths and then moving on to gateways. Finally streets and car parks are integrated into the training programme.

Important!
Remember not to ask too much of your dog. A basic trail always helps to preserve the dog's motivation and enjoyment.
It's up to you to assess how high you make your demands. How many times per week you train your dog is crucial.

Advanced learners

This stage is for dogs that have understood and have met the demands of the previously described tasks. It's essential that the dog has passed the previously described trails successfully. Consequently the training requirements can be increased.

- The trail should now be one to four hours old and 400 to 800 metres long.

- Vary the scent articles. Use for instance a piece of chewing gum or a bunch of keys.
- The trail should lead along water, through a little stream or across a bridge.
- The trail should lead over different surfaces such as in the city, the woods or a park.
- The trail should include several sharp turns.
- Don't put your dog on the trail right at the beginning. Let your dog sniff the scent article and let him find the starting point by

Crossing a little stream is already part of the advanced training. (Photo: Lehari)

Crossing wide streets or crossroads is part of the advanced training for man-trailing dogs. (Photo: Mozarski)

himself. Thereby you start at about 1 metre distance and increase it gradually. If the dog has always successfully completed the pri-ort asks further increased demands can be made.

- The trail should now be two to six hours old and 1.5 to 4.5 kilometres long.
- Look for an environment that is slightly contaminated.
- Include curves and outlets into the trail.
- The runner stays in certain places for a longer period of time. This is called a scent pool. The handler should know about this place to be able to observe the dog accurately in this situation.
- The trail crosses flowing water.
- The trail only leads over plastered areas. If all tasks have been performed by the team we continue.
- The trail should now be for to eight hours old and up to 6.5 kilometres long.
- The trail is laid by two runners who split up at some point (this is called splitting). At the end the right person must have been found. Start to work on this on soft ground.
- The runner should hide above the trail, for instance in a tree or a raised hide.
- The runner needs to be found in a crowd of people.
- The trail should lead across wide streets, a railway track or big crossings.

Summary

These exercises are one way of training the basics of man-trailing. There might be other ways but our training and the exchange of experiences have shown that this method provides a solid basic education.

I have deliberately not given a time limit for teaching the individual training steps. The learning process and the progress of the team depend on how often per week they are training and how much time can be invested. When a man-trailing team trains once a week small steps should be made. Only when the dog performs consistently over a longer period of time can the requirements be increased and new situations trained.

The dog needs to associate the scent articles with the individual smell of the person in order to be able to follow the trail. It's almost impossible to avoid minor transgressions from time to time. You should never lose your temper or interest. Check which are the underlying causes and don't fool yourself.

Always keep in mind that a dog isn't a machine that can be switched on and off arbitrarily. A dog is a unique living being that needs to be well-treated and well-understood to enjoy life with humans.

What does the dog tell us on a trail?

Body language and body expressions

Every dog has his own individual body language and works differently. When we observe the dog when hunting for game we notice that he is very determined and the hunt happens at a relentless pace. His attention is focused on grabbing the prey quickly. It's not about pottering about at every corner – the hunting and preying instinct demands an effective and fast job, done by going straight to the objective without making detours.

Here the dog never follows a track or a trail like on a railway track. During his search he constantly needs to eliminate other directions in the environment in order to follow his prey.

The dog's individual body parts and sense organs work together to form a constant body expression. This is part of the dog's disposition that we accept, encourage and train.

Following a human trail is neither a natural instinct nor is it in the dog's interest. The dog handler needs to teach him to do so first and then constantly reinforce and reward it.

The perception and the correct interpretation of his body expressions will be a factor in your success. The timing of the dog's reinforcement is crucial: it must happen at the right moment, at the right point. Immediate verbal praise for wanted and distinct behaviour is important, but the correction of the dog's unwanted behaviour needs to happen at the right moment as well. It's wise to correct verbally, such as, by saying, "Go on" or by making a harsh, rolled sound.

The correction should be clear and brief and be of a lower pitch. It's not advisable to correct the unwanted behaviour by jerking on the lead. If the lead gets tangled in the bushes later on or you need to stop the dog suddenly in a street he could regard this jerk as a correction and leave the trail.

When a dog constantly stops, sniffs at the same spot for a longer period of time or keeps marking on a trail the body expression is discontinued.

The dog might not be focused on his actual task or might have been distracted. He might even start overlapping onto other tracks. In this

For the handler it's important to interpret the dog's body expressions correctly when working a trail. (Photo: Mozarski)

case the dog handler needs to ask himself what is going on and intervene accordingly.

This dog reaches a railway track and determines whether the trail continues in this direction. On returning he gives a negative indication that means that the smell isn't to be found on the railway track. (Photos: Mozarski)

Negative indication on the trail

The negative indication is an instinctive disposition of the dog that results in his body expressions. It's an important indicator that we accept, encourage and train for working the trail.

While the dog is working a trail and is following the human scent he needs to eliminate the other directions of travel. We call this "negative indication". This kind of indication can be repeated constantly along a trail and is individual and differs from dog to dog. It demands an acute power of observation and the correct interpretation from the dog handler.

Negative indications can be very brief, for instance, just a head-turn. Some dogs, however, slow down their movements and look back when they smell that they can't move on.

When working a road junction or a turn-off the dog needs to check all directions to find out which way the missing person has gone. Some dogs walk in each direction and turn around when they don't find the trail there. Other dogs turn only a little in each direction, stop short and determine that the trail isn't going on that way. The dog handler needs to know how his trail partner works the trail and how he behaves.

With every form of indication and body expression that the dog displays, and that we recognize, mutual trust is built up and reinforced. When we tell the dog that his negative indication is positive information for us he won't get frustrated if he stops or loses a trail.

Circling at the beginning of the trail

The circle that the dog is drawing at the beginning of the trail is a positive indication. First he moves only slightly and it may even seem as if he isn't working. But then he suddenly changes direction, moving in a quick and tight circle. You will recognize this movement when he has filtered everything out and determined the direction of the trail. This is clearly visible unless you present the scent article to the dog scent before you put on the harness ("The present"). It's important to understand what the dog has just told you. With his body expression, the circling, he has filtered, checked and selected the whole area and now indicates the direction of the trail.

Sometimes it happens that the dog draws a starting circle that diverges from the course of the trail so far. In this case it could be that the dog has picked up some scent particles slightly beyond the trail. He first follows those particles and then comes across the further course of the trail. The dog, which has started in one direction, draws a circle in order to follow the trail in the right direction. This kind of movement tells the dog handler that he has worked out the course of the trail correctly.

As a dog handler you need to observe the dog's movements and reactions attentively all the time. With increasing trust, confidence builds up and dog and handler grow together as a team.

Circling on the trail

When the dog is drawing a circle while he is on the trail this body expression can have different meanings. The dog could have lost the direction of travel or even the trail itself. In these cases it's a negative indication. The circling movement also indicates that he is looking for the scent and is therefore concentrating on working. When he then pulls out of the circle and continues moving in a certain direction we know that he has found the trail. This kind of indication is positive for the handler. Such a positive indication after a negative indication lets you know that the dog has recovered the trail.

During the process you should neither stand in the dog's way nor hinder him. You should ideally try to stay behind the dog.

He also shouldn't be irritated by continual jerks on the lead as he could interpret every jerk as a correction. Let him continue working and observe him.

The circle the dog is drawing isn't necessarily symmetric in its movement, so it's very important to recognize this and understand its meaning. It can also happen that the dog slows

When the dog is drawing a circle on the trail he should not be irritated by jerking on the lead. (Photos: Lehari)

down noticeably before drawing the circle. This can make it more difficult for the handler to recognize the circling. Sometimes a dog also has the tendency to draw several circles – sort of drawing a double-circle – before he continues following the trail.

The zigzag assessment

This sort of movement is a negative indication. In order to spot the "middle course" of the trail the dog's head and forequarters move in a lateral zigzag pattern. This movement can be very abrupt. Through this negative elimination the dog can assure himself that the direction of the trail has neither changed to the left nor to the right.

This kind of body expression could mislead some handlers to presume that the dog is about to reach the end of the trail and is, so to speak, within the missing person's "scent cone". This could be possible but you should consider that the dog needs to perform this movement to eliminate the direction of travel to determine the actual course of his trail.

Wavy lines

The wavy line, or the curved way of moving, is very subtle and flowing. This forward motion is very similar to the zigzag assess-

A typical body expression when trailing is the zigzag movement in order to spot the correct "middle course" of the trail.
(Photos: Lehari)

ment in its performance. With the wavy movement the dog eliminates other directions in his surroundings in order to follow the actual course of the trail. This negative indication can easily be missed by the dog handler or misinterpreted because this body expression is so natural and inconspicuous. Dog handlers who have trained in the city may have already perceived this sort of movement.

How does the dog react when there is an access road turning off sideways? The dog briefly swings into this driveway and swings out again to find out whether the trail continues this way. His constantly flowing motion shows that he has eliminated this direction. At this point you know that the dog's concentration is still on the task and he is on the trail.

Some dogs can display this method of working the trail as a constant pattern. While you are observing the dog and recognizing the specific meaning of his body language you can picture the course of the trail worked so far as a map in your mind.

The head – turn

A sudden head-turn or other movement of the dog's head can have different meanings, as the following examples show.

A side road turns off the trail. When passing this road the dog briefly stops. He lifts up his head, turns it in this direction and briefly sniffs the air. Then he continues moving in the same direction as before and follows the course of the trail. This head-turn is a negative indication that eliminates wrong directions of travel. In this case the dog could also do a double – take, which means he turns his head in the wrong direction twice or has a longer glance into the street.

The course of the trail continues into a side road to your right. When passing this, the dog briefly turns his head into this street. Without further delay he continues moving in the same direction as before. Then he suddenly stops and turns round. He comes back, turns into the side road and follows the course of the trail. This previously performed brief and subtle head-turn into the street can be used as an indicator. First the dog has checked whether the scent matches the course in the previous direction. The stopping and turning round as a negative indication tell us that the person must have turned into the side road.

With his head movement the dog may have given us this piece of information before.

When the dog reaches an urban area with strange, strong smells such as exhaust fumes and rubbish, other observations can be made.

A dog approaches a store-front on his trail. He lifts up his head and turns it in a direction he doesn't take, however. He carries on, sticking to the direction of the actual trail. The dog is giving a negative indication and therefore has filtered out the fake scents.

The dog's head-turn can have different meanings. (Photo: Mozarski)

When the dog is in a crowded street with many pedestrians he will occasionally perform head-turns. His head turns in the direction of other people in order to eliminate them when searching for "his person".

Tail carriage

Every dog has an individual tail carriage that has an associated meaning. The tail can stick into the air just like an antenna, which for my dog, for instance, means that he is on the trail. With others the tail moves regularly but quietly from side to side. This can also mean being on the trail. A fast wagging movement could mean that the dog is close to the missing person. Whatever tail carriage your dog has and however he applies it in his work, its correct interpretation is one of the basic requirements in education and training.

Working old and fresh trails

When the dog has understood his task, older trails can be worked. I recommend slow progression in reference to the trail age. First train on trails that are one to five hours old before you work on overnight trails.

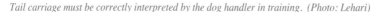

Tail carriage must be correctly interpreted by the dog handler in training. (Photo: Lehari)

Ask your trail runner to lay a trail in the morning. Start working on this trail with your dog after about one or two hours. This time span then is increased gradually.

The dog handler needs to know which body expressions the dog is displaying on an older trail. Dogs following older trails usually work more calmly and seem to be more focused than when on fresh trails. Many don't spend time on constantly monitoring the surroundings or checking on other people by doing head-turns. The nose could stick to the ground better than when searching a fresh trail.

When the dog is following an older trail and getting close to the end there could be a change. With the approach of the missing person the trail becomes fresher. The movements of the dog's whole body can get faster again. The dog handler must observe and recognize this difference between fresh and old trails.

The dog must learn always to filter out the freshest trail and follow it.

It's very important to observe and recognize all of the dog's individual body expressions. In the end you need to able to interpret them correctly. Only by intensive training and using known training trails can your powers of observation and your implementation skills be developed. During the training process you gain more and more experience and thereby inevitably learn to read your dog correctly. Your mutual trust grows constantly and welds you together into a successful man-trailing team.

This knowledge needs to be transferred to the whole trail and drawn into and used as a map in your mind. The dog handler always needs to be able to find his way. When the dog hesitates for one reason or another because he has lost or missed the trail or doesn't know how to continue, it's the dog handler's job to recognize the situation and intervene supportively. In addition he learns to locate the approximate course of the trail through his dog's body expressions.

How to continue

Recovering a trail

Recovering the trail becomes necessary when the dog isn't completely focused on the scent or is on the verge of totally losing the scent. The dog wants to work the trail but isn't really sure or shows insecurity. In this case the dog handler must support his dog. In this situation it's necessary to view the surroundings, to check the wind conditions or to recognize whether other conditions have changed. It's important not to hinder the dog when working and not to interrupt or disturb his movements.

This dog has understood everything and is waiting for the next task. (Photo: Mozarski)

The dog's behaviour and body expressions need to be carefully observed. When you see a glance in one direction but no further action or changes in motion you should step in supportively. Let the dog circle in the direction he was looking in. You can then observe him and see whether he is showing a reaction or can recover the trail there.

If you then also consider the wind conditions and the circumstances of the surroundings you can identify the actual course of the trail.

Recovery of a trail

It can happen that the dog loses a trail. In order that he can pick up the trail again you can use an effective handling technique. If the dog loses the course of the trail during training, stop him and verbally correct him. Then guide him back to the trail. Don't go back to the trail directly but rather approach it in a circling movement. Hold on tight to your dog's lead and correct him if he tries to pull. It's not until he has picked up the trail again and is heading in the right direction that you praise him verbally and allowhim to carry on following the trail.

The dog handler in this situation needs to recognize the dog's negative indication. That means he needs to know that the dog has lost the trail. Hoping to recover the trail, he goes back to the point where the dog was working it reliably.

Before you initiate the way back you should let the dog circle beyond this point at the spot where he seemed to lose the trail. It could be possible that for one reason or another the scent isn't present at this spot and therefore the trail is interrupted. The dog is now given the chance to search beyond this "scent gap" and possibly resume the trail.

It's important that you keep moving all the time while the dog is circling. Furthermore you should make sure that all possibilities and directions have been checked and eliminated.

Scent pool

What does the term "scent pool" mean? The easiest definition is:the accumulation of a scent at one place or point where the smell is stronger than on the trail itself.

This concentration of scent occurs when a person has stayed in one place for a longer period of time or is still situated in this place and constantly releases scent particles. When the person continues moving the scent is spread again and a trail that the dog can follow is generated. When the person stops, the quantity and the intensity of the scent particles increase. This is called "scent concentration".

The size and strength of the scent pool depend on how much time the person has spent on the spot and how old this scent pool is.

In a scent pool the smell is so overwhelming for the dog that he sometimes has problems finding the further course of the trail. (Photo: Lehari)

The surroundings have a direct effect on the formation of a scent pool. Natural boundaries and dips cause a stronger accumulation of scent particles whereas open spaces don't form a barrier and the scent can therefore spread out farther.

When the trail-layer has climbed up a hill this can cause an accumulation of scent at the bottom of the hill. Accumulation of humidity, nearby small waters or lakes can intensify the scent.

When a dog enters such a pool he can at first be confused and may circle around or double back along the trail, which is called a "backtrack" (see chapter Backtrack). Some dogs even stop working completely. The scent is so overwhelming that it can be very difficult for the dog to find the exit from this pool to carry on following the trail. It seems almost as if the dog is caught in a glass container.

When he can't get out of this scent pool by himself or is getting more and more confused when circling, start moving forwards out of the scent pool until he gives a negative indication again. Then search all directions systematically until the dog has recovered the course of the trail.

Something else happens when the person is still nearby, as in this case scent particles are still released continuously and the surroundings are drenched in the scent. This enormous concentration of scent can have an important effect on the dog. It's therefore not unusual even for the dog to pass the missing person several times. Depending on the area, the temperature and the humidity it can be that the accumulation of smell isn't situated immediately next to the person.

Let your dog work individually and don't try to influence him when he doesn't accept the missing person straight away.

Remember that the dog recognizes and identifies the person using his sense of smell, so what he sees is irrelevant. Put aside the thought that the dog also needs to see the person when you see and recognize the person. The picture that the dog has in his mind's eye develops on the basis of the person's individual scent through his sense of smell.

Therefore don't train only in the daytime but also particularly in the dark. The dog outperforms us in this respect, so it makes no difference to him whether it's light or dark because of his sense of smell and orientation. The difficulties relate to the dog handler, whose vision is limited in the dark. Consequently he has to rely on his dog completely.

It's important to train for scent pools and to learn how the dog recognizes and shows us them as such. Scent pools are created and practised in training under controlled circumstances. Don't underestimate the difficulty of working a scent pool. It can take more time than working the course of a trail.

Make the scent-pool training simple but effective. This should be carried out as follows. The whole trail is quite short. A scent pool is created with only a short trail leading out of the pool so that the person can be found easily. The focus is clearly on practising the scent pool.

Implementation in an emergency

When the man-trailer enters a scent pool in an emergency and isn't able to find his way out, don't be misled into thinking that your dog has lost the trail of the missing person or the criminal. The person could still be nearby. Some influences prevent the dog from identifying the person directly but he can show you that the person has to be close by.

If this is a wanted criminal, ask for support from your colleagues or even a protection dog, as safety is paramount.

If you are looking for a missing person who might be injured or lying somewhere in a confused state the use of square-search dogs as additional support is strongly advised. Priority must be given to the fast location of the injured person and immediate medical care.

In an emergency it's important to find the missing person quickly and to look after her immediately. (Photo: Lehari)

When the dog follows the actual course of the trail and not the decoy track he is praised verbally but should continue trailing immediately. (Photo: Lehari)

Crossing and splitting

The next step is to teach the dog scent discrimination. In this the trail is run by at least two people.

As soon as the dog is performing well and has the confidence to go trailing with the aid of only a person's scent article you can start integrating a decoy track into the trail. This entails a decoy crossing the actual course of the trail. The crossing happens at about the same time as the trail is laid.

It's important for the dog handler to know where the decoy has crossed the trail. Let your dog work out the new situation for himself when he reaches the spot. Observe your dog and how he copes with it. Some dogs might not even be interested in the decoy track and might continue to follow the right trail.

In this case the dog is praised verbally. Other dogs might stay longer at the decoy track and further investigate it. Give your dog enough time without intervening prematurely. Only when the dog seems to be in serious difficulty give him extra support, but you shouldn't guide him or harshly correct him.

When the dog is tempted to follow the decoy track, just stand still while giving a soft "No" command and start moving rhythmically back to the right trail. The dog needs to feel as if he has resolved the difficulty. Praise him verbally as soon as he starts heading in the right direction.

The same method and technique is used when splitting a trail. In this case two people

Splitting

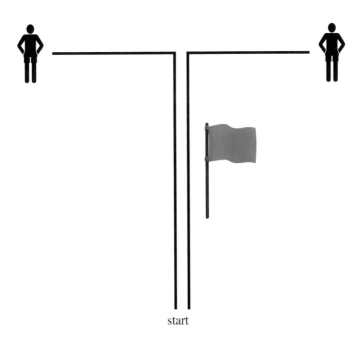

start

start walking next to each other at the same time. After about 50 metres they split up and continue in different directions. Observe the same rules as before for the crossing of a trail.

Backtrack

The trail-layer walks in a straight line for about 50 metres. Then he makes a 180-degree turn and walks back the same way. After about 20 metres he makes a sharp turn to the left or right and continues walking. Whether he turns left or right depends on the wind direction. The dog should by no means be able to smell the scent through the air, and the runner shouldn't be visible to the dog.

This is dog training, so the dog handler is informed about the course of the trail before training and has the chance to observe his dog.

Backtrack

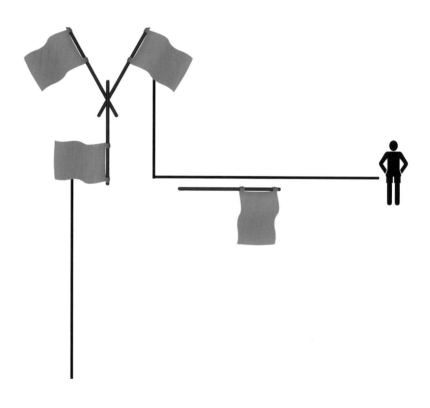

Depending on the dog's training stage and his motivation he should continue walking straight ahead and reach a point beyond the trail. He might not realize that the scent is getting weaker or he may circle to eliminate the other direction with a negative indication. If the dog continues walking straight ahead beyond the trail the dog handler needs to give him extra support.

In this case the dog is stopped and he gets the verbal cue "No". Remember that the dog is brought into a completely new situation here. The dog needs to feel that he has solved the problem and achieved the objective successfully. Therefore the dog handler should be patient and encourage the dog to keep looking for the further course of the trail.

The dog handler therefore guides the dog or lets him circle back to the point of intersection where the person changed direction. Now the dog handler can see the dog's reaction and find out whether he picks up and follows the further course of the trail. The dog is praised verbally at the right moment and at the right spot.

Dogs that start circling at the end of the straight line and start giving negative indications are praised for this behaviour, as the dog is communicating information to the handler that the situation has changed.

The dog himself has worked and mastered this new situation and difficulty. The dog handler must only make sure that the dog doesn't wear himself out completely. As soon as the dog shows signs of frustration and asks for help the handler for help intervenes supportively.

In order to offer the dog a positive end to the training session it's wise to add a short basic trail.

Line-up

In a line-up several people are positioned in a row from which a certain person is to be identified by the dog. The line-up is an exercise that trains scent discrimination and identification of a person.

You can arrange this exercise as follows. Three to four people walk a distance of at least 40 metres from the starting point together. Then they split up into different directions in a fan-shape. From this splitting point every person walks about another 80 metres and stops so that they are still visible. The people are separated by a distance of about 30 to 40 metres.

The dog is put on the trail at the starting point with one of the people's scent article. Now he should follow the right trail and identify the missing person.

Step 1
This exercise can be built up with a basic trail. In this case you position two or three people at the end of the trail about 30 metres apart, as described above, but still visible. The person

to be identified starts walking from the starting point, where she can be observed by the dog, and also positions herself at a distance of about 30 metres from the other people. As soon as she reaches her destination the dog is launched.

The position of the person is changed within the exercises to be undertaken. When the dog has understood the task the individual missing person changes too, so that the dog doesn't focus on one special person but is actually driven by the scent. The dog needs the confidence to be able to identify one person out of a group.

Step 2

In the second step the exercise is carried out just as in step 1. The person walks away from the starting point observably but then the dog is led away so that he can't observe and follow the remainder of the exercise. When the runner has reached his position at the appropriate distance from the other people, the dog is led back to the starting point and the scent article. This exercise also is practised with different people from the group.

Step 3

When the dog has understood steps 1 and 2 and performed them successfully over a period of time you can increase the requirements as follows. The people position themselves while the dog isn't present. Only after all the runners have positioned themselves

the dog is led to the training ground and launched.

Not until the dog has successfully performed this task can you slowly start reducing the distance between the people. Then you can also vary the schedule: launch the dog 10 to 15 minutes later. The people can also position themselves at different times.

Negative indication at the beginning and the end of a trail

This exercise should only be trained with the dog when he really has worked different trails confidently and consistently over a longer period of time. Young dogs or dogs that are not confident enough can get confused or frustrated with this new exercise. Don't fool yourself, and make a decision for the good of the dog.

The negative indication at the beginning of a trail must be trained separately with the dog but should never be provided as the final exercise of a training day. In this the dog is presented the scent article of a corresponding person who isn't, and never has been, close by. The dog is launched as usual by pre-scenting, harnessing and starting. Now let the dog check which direction the person ran in. Give him enough time and observe him carefully no matter if he circles once or several times. It's the dog handler's job to support the dog at the right moment. Some dogs might be very confused and wander about enquiringly. As soon as the dog looks at his owner in this way he is praised and supported.

The decision about which form of indication the dog should show must be made by the dog handler. Either he jumps on the handler or he sits in front of him. Just stick to one of those forms of indication. It always depends on the dog how he behaves and what he offers the dog handler. Some dogs might sit down by themselves after a while. Then they are praised immediately.

Give your dog a radius of the whole length of the lead – about 12 metres – in each direction. He should satisfy himself thoroughly that there is no trail nearby that matches the scent article. After completion of this task always follow with a basic trail.

In later emergencies there will be many trails where the missing person can't be found. In this case we have a negative indication at the end of the trail. The person may, for example, have got into a car and driven away. The dog handler now needs to recognize which circumstances indicate that the person can't be found.

In the following a training process is described where a person has left in a car.

The runner walks along a street that leads him to his car. He gets into his car and drives away. The trail can be about 50 to 100 metres long. The dog is launched at the starting point and works the trail. Observe your dog's behaviour when he has reached the point of disappearance. Let him investigate this point thoroughly. In doing so he shouldn't go too far beyond the destination. Give him the full length of the lead to search the area. As soon as the dog has realized that the trail doesn't continue and shows that he doesn't know what has happened it's your turn as the dog handler again. You can train the same form of indication as before with the negative start. The dog either jumps up on you or sits down to show you that the trail has ended. The dog is rewarded generously for this information.

Contamination

When the training area contains a range of different smells we refer to it as a "contaminated area". As a beginner the dog should be trained in an area with as few unfamiliar, strong smells as possible. Therefore we first work a person's fresh trails. Later on in training we increasingly work on trails that are older than the smells in the area.

Contamination can arise from different people in the area, such as, in parks or shopping streets, or at places of interest.

Training should also take place in areas with a lot of game. Train near a farm or a riding stable, near meadows and in places where many dog handlers walk their dogs.

Strong smells that could influence the dog are found at petrol stations and in busy streets. Heating and air conditioning systems can also cause disturbance. Practise in these strongly contaminated areas and observe your dog's reactions.

The more advanced the dog, the more contaminated with other smells the training area may be. This is how he learns to recognize the missing person's individual smell. (Photo: Lehari)

The essentials in brief

- Before every training session you should make a plan and record the training accordingly.
- Training should be carried out continuously.
- Introduce a routine for training.
- Take your time and be calm when training.
- Small, continuous steps lead to success.
- The start should always be carried out quietly in the same way.
- The starting command should only be given once when presenting the scent article.
- Keep changing the starting direction. It should not always lead into the same direction as the course of the trail.
- Keep changing places and surroundings of the training area.
- Keep changing the scent articles.
- Stop your dog on the trail and introduce breaks in which he can drink out of his water bowl.
- New situations must be planed and practised.
- Don't undertake experiments at the expense of the dog.
- The dog should only be praised and motivated at the right moment when working the trail. Unnecessary chattiness should be stopped.
- The dog should always have that the feeling that he has worked the trail and has been successful.
- The dog should be supported by the dog handler if necessary.
- The dog should never be restricted, guided or led.
- Be careful with done too quickly corrections. This concerns unconscious and conscious body language and leash corrections.

- Be careful with corrections at crossings. Approach the crossing slowly, almost stop and wait until the dog has worked it out and continue following the trail.
- Don't always just run after your dog. Find out whether it is the direction of the trail. In this case you can deliberately distract the dog.
- Position decoys on the trail.
- Be careful with indicated trails. Don't intervene too quickly just because you know the actual course of the trail.
- Keep changing the trail layers in respect of the quarries.
- Keep integrating difficulties into the trail, such as scent pools or backtracks.
- The runner can use a vehicle such as a bicycle, rollerblades or a car maybe even a horse with experienced dogs.

- "Celebrate" and reward your dog extensively after finding the person. Don't wait too long before doing so. A positive completion is very important for the dog.
- Keep varying between fresh and old tracks.
- The runner should be found in different positions – sitting down, lying, in a tree, hidden and so on.
- Practise on as many different surfaces as possible. Those should merge, such as from a forest into a residential area.
- With increasing experience and performance you should start integrating negative trails.
- Practise and train with an assistant who doesn't know the course of the trail.
- Don't ask too much of your dog.
- Always trust your dog!

Bibliography

Coren, Stanley
The Intelligence of Dogs: A Guide to the
Thoughts, Emotions and Inner Lives of our
Canine Companions
Free Press

Davis, Terry
Scent articles, key of success 1998
Virginia Bloodhound search and
rescue association
Publication on the internet

Kocher, Kevin and Monroe-Kocher, Robin
Read any training or tracking dog
www. bloodhoundtraining.com

Kocher, Kevin and Monroe-Kocher, Robin
Scent article
www. bloodhoundtraining.com

Kocher, Kevin and Monroe-Kocher, Robin
Training for backtracks
www. bloodhoundtraining.com

Lutenberg, John and Porter, Linda
A practical guide to training
and working a trailing dog
USA

Masson, Jeffrey
Dogs Never Lie About Love:
Reflections On The Emotional World Of Dogs
Three Rivers Press

Senger, Daniel
Scentpool
USA

Shuler, Jack
Tracking versus Mantrailing
www.jackshuler.com

Shuler, Jack and Grist, Behesha
Seminarunterlagen Mantrailing I, Juni 2004

Syrotuck, W.
Hund, Geruch und Fährte
Deutsche Ausgabe Dr Weidner Eigenverlag